The Lost Art of Confrontation

From Conflict to Connection

Daniel T. Newton

© Copyright 2023 Daniel Newton, GP Publishing

www.GracePlaceRedding.com

Contributing authors: Downing McDade, Austin Chappell, Elizabeth Newton, Amyjoy Osinga and the Grace Place Leadership Team.
ISBN: 978-1-957601-11-3

All rights reserved. This book is protected by the copyright laws of the United States of America. This book may not be copied or reprinted for commercial gain or profit. The use of short quotations or occasional page copying for personal or group study is permitted and encouraged.

Unless otherwise identified, all Scripture is from the New King James Version®. Copyright © 1982 by Thomas Nelson. Used by permission. All rights reserved.

Scripture taken from the Holy Bible, NEW INTERNATIONAL VERSION®, NIV® Copyright © 1973, 1978, 1984, 2011 by Biblica, Inc.® Used by permission. All rights reserved worldwide.

Scripture quotations marked (NLT) are taken from the Holy Bible, New Living Translation, copyright © 1996, 2004, 2007, 2013, 2015 by Tyndale House Foundation. Used by permission of Tyndale House Publishers, Inc., Carol Stream, Illinois 60188. All rights reserved.

Resources by Daniel Newton and Grace Place Ministries:
Truth in Tension: 55 Days to Living in Balance
Immeasurable: Reviewing the Goodness of God
Never Give Up: The Supernatural Power of Christlike Endurance
The Lost Art of Discipleship
The Lost Art of Discipleship Workbook
The Lost Art of Perseverance
All Things
It Is Finished
The Lost Art of Faith Righteousness
The Lost Art of Fasting
The Lost Art of Selfless Love
The Lost Art of Rest
The Lost Art of Excellence
The Lost Art of Friendship
The Lost Art of Confrontation
GP Music: Beginnings – Worship Album
For more information on these books
and other inspiring resources, visit us at
www.GracePlaceMedia.com

Table of Contents

Introduction	1
Part 1: Biblical Confrontation	5
Chapter 1: Love is Confrontational	7
Chapter 2: The Truth About Confrontation	13
Chapter 3: It's All About Love	17
Part 2: The Fruit of Confrontation	23
Chapter 4: Heart Transformation	25
Chapter 5: Creating Relational Depth	29
Chapter 6: Grace to Change	35
Part 3: Confronting	39
Chapter 7: Bringing Awareness	41
Chapter 8: What to Do When Confronted	45
Chapter 9: No One-Size-Fits-All	51
Conclusion	57

Introduction

Confrontation is for everyone. Regardless of experience or position, everyone, at some point in their life, will run into a problem or issue they will need to address. Conflict is inevitable, but it doesn't have to be the end of the world. When handled well, adversity becomes the gateway to deeper connection.

For many today, "confrontation" is a scary or even dirty word. Perhaps you saw the cover of this book and your mind immediately flashed to images of yelling, screaming, or meltdowns. You might have been raised in a house where that was the "normal" way to handle disagreements. First, there is nothing normal about yelling and screaming. Secondly, this is not the kind of confrontation I'm talking about. However, if you had that mental image, you're probably not alone.

Many people today are in one of two extremes. Some believe the only way to truly address issues is by raising their voice or being intense. Others choose to be silent about things that need to be spoken up about. We in the church have been especially silent, believing in a false image of a passive Jesus. We picture Him as a meek little lamb who got along with everybody, forgetting that He was also a bold lion. We have bought into the thinking that acting like Jesus means never speaking up or rocking the boat. This is a lie, and the world around us is showing the fruit of our passivity.

It's no secret that our world is suffering from an identity crisis. Turn on any TV station right now, and you'd most likely hear a story about men winning trophies in women's sports, kids being taken to drag queen story hour at the local library, movies, music videos, and awards shows being flooded with blatant satanism, etc. Some might ask, "How did we get here?" The answer is simple—by staying quiet when it was time to speak up.

The Bible tells us it is "the little foxes that spoil the vines" (Song of Sol. 2:15), meaning that the little things we don't address have the potential to disrupt or ruin our fruitfulness. When we leave problems unaddressed, the problems don't go away. They become larger. Little compromises left unchecked become larger ones.

What if the people passing these laws and pushing these agendas had someone much earlier on in their lives confronting the small compromises they were making? What might be different in the world today?

I'm not saying confrontation would have solved everything going on, but I can guarantee you things would look a lot different. I know this because what you don't confront, you condone. If no one does anything to change a situation, the situation will stay the same. As the saying goes, the only thing necessary for the triumph of evil is for good men to do nothing.

However, there is good news. If not speaking up is what got us into this mess, learning to confront can get us out. Confrontation might have become a lost art in our culture, but it doesn't need to stay that way.

Introduction

This book is designed to re-present confrontation as God intended because, contrary to many teachings found today, confrontation *is* Biblical. The Bible is full of teaching on how to address issues with those around us, and, ultimately, how to live in right relationship with both God and others.

I believe that when our judgments, bad perspectives, and negative past experiences with conflict are removed, we will be able to see clearly the great benefits we can gain from boldly addressing problems and issues. There is power in living in a culture of confrontation. When we learn to speak the truth in love, it creates unity, aligning us around commonly held values.

It doesn't matter how you were raised or what your background is. *Anyone* can learn how to confront with peace, respect, and confidence. It's time the Lost Art of Confrontation becomes found!

Part I

Biblical Confrontation

"We should no longer be children, tossed to and fro and carried about with every wind of doctrine, by the trickery of men, in the cunning craftiness of deceitful plotting, but, speaking the truth in love, may grow up in all things into Him who is the head— Christ— from whom the whole body, joined and knit together by what every joint supplies, according to the effective working by which every part does its share, causes growth of the body for the edifying of itself in love."

- Ephesians 4:14-16

Chapter 1

Love is Confrontational

Confrontation is one of the primary vehicles for creating discipline and maturity in our Christian walk. Without it, we could continue to be like little children, tossed around by every new teaching and doctrine that comes along, unable to walk securely in the love and confidence Christ desires for us.

We are called to be disciples of Jesus. The word disciple means "disciplined one." How is discipline developed? It is developed through our actions and thought patterns being tested and challenged until they are brought into alignment with scripture—a process that begins with our loving Father.

Depending on your background, viewing God as a disciplinarian might sound intimidating or painful. However, God is both confrontational *and* loving—and these two ideas are not contradictory. From God's perspective, the fact He chooses to confront us is proof that He loves us (see Heb. 12:6).

In other words, the fact that He holds us to account, addresses issues, calls us higher, and refines us is all evidence that He views us as sons and daughters. We should actually be more worried if we were not experiencing any form of discipline or correction from the Lord, because, as Hebrews says, this would mean we're not part of the family.

Because God loves us and has called us to be like Him, He confronts the areas where we are immature. This is actually evidence of His goodness at work in our lives. However, if we're unfamiliar with what God's goodness actually looks like, we might be confused when He begins correcting our actions and behaviors. We could mistakenly think He is upset with us, when in fact He is actively making us more into His image.

It's dangerous when people teach the goodness of God without truly knowing what His goodness is like. We often fall into the trap of basing our perception of Jesus on an incomplete picture of His interactions with others. As I said earlier, many people today see Jesus as the little lamb who never broke a bruised reed. However, Jesus also rebuked his disciples for their lack of faith when they woke Him up to calm a storm (Luke 8:25).

Yes, Jesus did say "Come to me all you are weary and heavy leaden," but He also said to Peter, "Get behind Me, Satan! You are an offense to Me, for you are not mindful of the things of God, but the things of men" (Matt. 16:23). What some may have a difficult time seeing is that *all* of these examples show His goodness.

Problems arise when we try to define God's love by what modern human standards say "feels" loving, instead of what *is* loving. Many times, true love being expressed doesn't always leave you *feeling* loved. To the child, it doesn't feel loving when a parent snatches their hand away from putting the paper clip in the electrical socket. However, to the parent, that is an act of love by saving the child's life.

It probably didn't "feel" good when Jesus questioned the disciples' faith or rebuked Peter for partnering with Satan. Yet, looking at their lives, we can see that these moments taught them something that God used to correct their heart motivations and ultimately, bear great fruit in their lives.

We're not called to live according to our feelings, regardless of whether they are good or bad. Everything must be based upon the truth established in His Word. Sometimes, love is a comforting word spoken in a moment of mourning or loss. Other times, love is an aggressive act of snatching someone away from fire. One is not greater than the other. And throughout the Word, God shows us examples of both.

His love for us and His voice of confrontation cannot be separated. He loves us, and therefore He corrects us. When He corrects us, we know He loves us. Let's look at a few examples of God confronting in scripture.

After the very first instance of sin in Genesis 3, God immediately addressed the problem. He didn't leave Adam and Eve alone saying, "Oh, they know they're wrong. I pray they'll figure it out." No! He called to Adam in the garden to ask what happened. Adam chose a shameful and blame-shifting response, but nevertheless, God confronted the issue.

When David slept with Bathsheba and murdered Uriah, God sent a prophet to confront him. God used a story of another person being mistreated and abused to awaken David's conscience to his own hypocrisy. Doing this exposed David's sin and brought upon him judgment. When David responded with genuine humility, God forgave him.

God used Elijah to confront the wicked king Ahab in 1 Kings 18. When Ahab saw Elijah, he said, "'Is it you, o troubler of

Israel?'" (1 Kings 18:17) Elijah responded that Ahab was the real one causing trouble for the nation because He followed after the sins of his fathers. Long before any punishment came, there was first a confrontation of Ahab's sin and wickedness.

These are just a few examples of times God intervened to confront and correct His people. Because so many have discomfort around the topic of confrontation, we have not been trained to see how prevalent it is in God's character. Throughout Scripture, God speaks against unrighteousness. When unrighteousness is confronted, it's always meant to be a course correction.

These interactions are illustrations of what God's relationship with us is like. However, no picture of God is painted more perfectly than when He came into the world as Jesus Christ.

Jesus specifically says in Luke 6:17, "Take heed to yourselves. If your brother sins against you, rebuke him; and if he repents, forgive him." In other words, if someone does something wrong to you, Jesus charges us to confront them. He also stood boldly against the religious leaders. When they were prideful and legalistic, He called them a den of vipers. When the disciples didn't know what to do, after they had seen Jesus perform many miracles, He confronted them saying they were a twisted generation.

Scripture is clear. When we do something wrong, God is faithful to let us know. He disciplines us. He shows us how what we did was not according to our nature in Him. As we yield to His correction and change our ways, we grow and become more like Him. He doesn't correct us to punish us. He does it because He loves us. In the same way, we're charged to restore someone who's gone into sin with a spirit of gentleness and to stand up for what is right.

Love is Confrontational

Despite what you may have seen or experienced in your own life, being loving and confrontational are not enemies or opposites. In God, we see both expressed as two sides of the same coin. God fully loves us for where we are, and, in the same moment, invites to to be refined more into the image of Jesus. He meets us where were are and calls us higher still.

This is what it means to engage in true confrontation—to meet someone where they are, to seek to understand, to address an issue, and to call them higher. When we confront in this way, we are not only helping out our fellow brothers and sisters, but we are actively engaging with the heart of God.

Chapter 2

The Truth About Confrontation

If confrontation needs to be redefined and reintroduced into the body of Christ, it begs the question: what exactly *is* confrontation? Confrontation is addressing, questioning, or challenging something that you see as off with the goal of bringing the person to the truth which leads them to greater freedom. Read the last sentence again and think about the three words *addressing, questioning,* and *challenging*. None of these have to be intense, loud, or in your face. It's not manipulative or shaming. Often, it begins with a simple question or desire to understand.

When I say confrontation is addressing something that you see as "off," what does that mean? Sometimes, you may not be able to pinpoint the exact problem causing friction in a situation, but you may feel that there was something unusual about what someone said or did. This unusualness is what I call being "off." It is any interaction where you walk away thinking, *That was a strange way to respond*, or *What was that about?* While it may feel slight, simply calling something out as being off can be the doorway into a deeper conversation about what's going on in someone's heart.

Confrontation is simply designed to open the door for transformation to take place, however, it is not the transformation itself. The Holy Spirit is the only one who has the ability to create lasting change in someone's heart. Our responsibility is to partner with Him in bringing something to light and then letting the Lord do the rest.

Confrontation is about looking at the root. This is why it's so important that we never prejudge someone, thinking we know the reason behind what they're doing. Sometimes, the root of why someone is acting a certain way is surprising. Yes, the person might have sinned, but what led them down that path in the first place?

James 1:14-15 says, "But each one is tempted when he is drawn away by his own desires and enticed. Then, when desire has conceived, it gives birth to sin." What this shows us is that no believer who loves Jesus just wakes up one day and decides to sin. We have to be drawn away and enticed. We can learn a lot by asking someone, "What led to this decision? How did you get here?" This takes us beyond the sinful action and begins to reveal what's really been going on in the person's heart that opened them up to choosing sin over righteousness.

This is an important distinction because, in discipleship, we never want to be pruning behaviors. This is what religion does. When all we do is spend time correcting people's actions, we end up creating a culture of performers. People's actions might change, but their hearts will remain unaffected. Give it time, and the dysfunction at the root will manifest itself in some other way until the true root has been dealt with. However, when the root of an issue is addressed, *all* of the outward manifestations—even ones we might not have noticed yet—will stop. This is why confrontation is powerful when done well—it opens up a way for the Lord to deal with the heart of the matter.

Our hearts are like a garden. If you've ever tried to weed a garden, you'll know that the easiest weeds to deal with are the small ones. If you catch them when they're small, they're easily pulled up by hand. However, when the root is allowed to sink in and go deep, it's a much harder process.

Many of the lies that we believe look or sound silly when brought into the light. When we live in a culture where confrontation is normal, lies and deception get exposed quickly. They are never able to become deeply rooted.

The Lord's presence and His Word are light. 1 John 1:7 tells us, "But if we walk in the light as He is in the light, we have fellowship with one another, and the blood of Jesus Christ His Son cleanses us from all sin." We are called to let the light of the Lord's Word and presence invade every area of our lives. When we withhold parts of ourselves—our thoughts, choices, beliefs, etc.—from being exposed to the light of the Lord, we are creating places where things can grow in darkness.

Lies and deception are like a fungus. They require darkness and isolation to grow, and the longer we allow offense or judgments to grow in darkness, the bigger they will become. Through addressing, questioning, and challenging, confrontation brings to light the lies we believe. This allows us to see them clearly for what they are and robs them of their power. When we expose the lies we believe to the truth and power of the Word of God, they begin to lose their grip.

Often, when we are under the influence of lies, we tend to lose our grip on reality. Because no one is addressing or calling out problems, we get lulled into a false sense of security, thinking everything is totally fine. This illustrates both the danger of isolation and the incredible power of confrontation. Confrontation is a wake-up call. It shakes us out of fantasy land and forces us to come to grips with the decisions we're making and how we're living.

It's so important that we never compromise on telling the truth and living according to it. The Word is the foundation of the life of every believer. It should feel wrong to be comfortable knowing the truth and letting people we care about walk around trapped in fantasy land. Never value relationship above speaking the truth because, ultimately, the best relationships are those where truth is the foundation.

This is the reason why confrontation is such a vital part of a thriving church community. Often, we want to go to the next level, but we can't see on our own what has been holding us back. I believe that most people would genuinely want to be free of their issues if they could clearly see either what the problems were or how much they were affecting their lives.

Many believers stay trapped in their issues because people around them stay silent. However, love speaks up. Love shares the truth. Love covers a multitude of sins. The Bible doesn't say love lets a multitude of sins slide. Love is vocal, passionate, and committed to letting the light of God shine brightly.

When we are surrounded by a loving community that is committed to identifying anything hindering growth, confrontation will be a normal discipline. We will not spend time needlessly going around the mountain, making the same mistakes over and over. We will be able to clearly identify where we need help and where we need God to correct our broken perspectives. Only then will we be able to grow, mature, and move forward.

Chapter 3

It's All About Love

If confrontation is an act of love, then love may not always look how we think it should. The world portrays love as butterflies in your stomach or moonlight and roses. It comes with the phrase, "I wouldn't want to do anything to hurt this person." We think saying something that might rub someone the wrong way is unloving, but when we do this, we unknowingly build a fear of speaking up.

However, the moment we change our perspective to see giving and receiving correction as how we build connection, we will begin to see greater growth and deeper relationships. Ephesians 4:14 tells us, "But, speaking the truth in love, may [we] grow up in all things into Him who is the head—Christ—." The very thing so many of us are afraid to do, speak the truth, is the very thing that causes growth and maturity.

Notice that it's not simply about speaking the truth. If you've been on social media recently, you'll know we live in a world where people are constantly speaking "the truth", but the fruit is hatred and division. If we come into a situation and start tearing someone apart about their motives and issues, we run the risk of destroying the person rather than building them up. The truth outside of the context of love can be one of the most destructive forces on the planet.

The Lord wants us to speak the truth *in love*. When we confront someone and share the truth because we love them, it has a completely different effect. When paired with the love of God, speaking the truth is one of the most constructive and encouraging ways to see someone come into the fullness of Christ. Godly confrontation is an act of love, and love is not passive.

Love fights. It comes down into someone's mess to look them in the eyes and help pull them out. It doesn't allow someone to continue walking around with their mind stuck in negative cycles. It brings understanding and calls them to their created purpose.

If someone is not seeing the truth, there has to be a passion burning in us to say, "This might be where you are at, but I don't want to leave you here. I love you. I'm going to fight for you and fight for the truth in your life to the best of my ability." This is what it looks like to be a part of the family of God. Selfless love and commitment create an environment where confrontation thrives.

Commitment creates a sense of safety that opens people up to listen. When people understand that you are for them, that you are on their side, that you treat them like family, and that you are fighting for them like family, confrontation becomes easier to navigate. As the old saying goes, people don't care what you know until they know how much you care. When someone knows that you love them and that you are confronting them for their good and not your own, the conversation will always go more peacefully.

Without love, confrontation will be powered by selfish ambition, which can manifest itself as control, manipulation, annoyance, frustration without resolve, judgments, or taking things personally. The key to a healthy confrontation is establishing yourself in a heart of love in the midst of every conflict. This doesn't mean you coddle or baby someone. People can sense when they are respected and cared for. Where there's respect there's openness.

You might ask, what is the best way to overcome the fear of confronting someone? The answer is simple—don't make it about you. When you can see and understand how much God loves the other person, confrontation will go much easier. All confrontation is meant to be an overflow of seeing God's love for the person in front of you. When you see someone through His eyes, you will naturally want the best for them.

1 John 4:20 says, "If someone says, 'I love God,' and hates his brother, he is a liar; for he who does not love his brother whom he has seen, how can he love God whom he has not seen?" What John is communicating is that it is impossible to truly love God and not also love your brother. Jesus gave a new commandment to His disciples in John 13:34-35, "A new commandment I give to you, that you love one another; as I have loved you, that you also love one another. By this all will know that you are My disciples, if you have love for one another."

Jesus wanted His disciples to love others the exact way He loved them. The amazing thing is that Jesus regularly rebuked and confronted His disciples, which shows us that we should do the same. In order to be known as His disciples, we have to get over our fear of confrontation and realize we are confronting for the sake of others.

The Lost Art of Confrontation

So much of the fear we experience when thinking about confrontation stems from our own negative past experiences with either being confronted or trying to confront someone else. Instead of taking it before the Lord to learn what should have been done differently, we swing to an extreme, saying things like "*all* confrontation is bad" instead of "*that* confrontation was bad." All this does is stunt our spiritual growth and normalize dysfunction. Then, the next time we find ourselves in a similar situation, we seek to please the person rather than speaking the truth that could set them free (John 8:32).

There is only one way to truly conquer being afraid of confrontation—do it! This is the only way we will ever be able to experience that the fear and insecurity we felt for so long was simply false evidence appearing real. When you have someone else's best interest at heart and they know you love and respect them, there is nothing to fear. They may disagree, but it is far more likely they will hear what you have to say and take it before the Lord. They never get the opportunity to grow if you choose to say nothing.

Part II

The Fruit of Confrontation

"A word fitly spoken is like apples of gold
In settings of silver.
Like an earring of gold and an ornament of fine gold
Is a wise rebuker to an obedient ear."
- Proverbs 25:11-12

Chapter 4

Heart Transformation

It's important that we have a correct perspective and expectation of what is supposed to happen in a confrontation. We, as human beings, have no ability to bring transformation or healing to someone's heart. The only one who can truly change a heart is the Lord. In confrontation, this means we are not the heart surgeon. That role belongs to the Lord. We are simply acting as the scalpel He uses to make the incision.

Addressing something and bringing it to light is the *beginning* of a process that ends with the Lord changing our hearts. This means that the cutting open, or the revealing of the issue, is only the first step. It is the invitation into healing, not the healing itself. So then, what is supposed to happen next?

Psalm 147:3 says, "He heals the brokenhearted and binds up their wounds." *He* heals. *He* binds up. You're not responsible for orchestrating change in someone's life. All you can do is speak up when you see something that is off. The rest is up to the person to take before the Lord.

If you're confronted about something, you have been given a responsibility. You need to get alone with the Lord, to get to the root of why your behavior or thinking has gotten off course, and to ask Him to change you. This is the only way confrontation is effective.

There is a myth that transformation happens with the passing of time. We perceive that people just naturally get more mature as they get older, but that's not the case at all. Maturity is not a by-product of age and does not happen by accident. Maturity happens through willingly dealing with the issues in our lives that hold us back from all of what God has called us to be. There are no shortcuts. It only comes through a conscious decision to make a change and leave the childish things behind.

As a mentor and a spiritual father, whenever I confront someone I'm leading, I have certain expectations. I expect the person to go to the Lord, work out what's been going on, and come back to me so we can resolve it. This is an important step because not all confrontations are resolved in the moment.

If there's a bigger issue where the person is having a difficult time seeing what you're bringing up, they might have to talk to the Lord, get revelation, and then come back to finish the conversation. In a culture where confrontation and addressing issues is normal, this should be the expected result.

When we operate in this way, it takes the pressure off of the confrontation itself. We don't need to have answers or solutions to solve whatever the person might be going through. We're simply pinpointing something off and trusting the Lord to work within the other person to resolve whatever might be going on. As I said earlier, we often have no idea what might be the true root behind someone's actions or perspective, but the Lord always does. When confrontation is done well, it opens the door for truth to come in, and for the Lord to speak the truth they need to be set free.

Heart Transformation

When you are confronted with a problem or issue in your life, you have the choice to continue living the way you were or to do something differently. In order to change what you're *doing*, you have to change the way you're *thinking*.

I like the quote, "Your thoughts are the preview of your life's coming attractions." The way you think about a problem will inevitably show up in your life and actions. Romans 12:2 (NIV) says, "Do not conform to the pattern of this world, but be transformed by the renewing of your mind. Then you will be able to test and approve what God's will is—His good, pleasing and perfect will".

The word transformed here is the Greek word *metamorphoo*. It means "to change into another form, to transform, to transfigure". In order to stop doing something that's harmful you actually have to become something different. You can't keep thinking the same way and expect to get a different result. So, how do you change your mind? You have to take a higher thought. Isaiah writes, "'For My thoughts are not your thoughts, Nor are your ways My ways,' says the Lord. 'For as the heavens are higher than the earth, So are My ways higher than your ways, And My thoughts than your thoughts'" (Is. 55:8-9). God's thoughts are higher than ours. God's desire for us is to be conformed into the image of Jesus (see Rom. 8:29). This involves thinking like Him. The way we become acquainted with His thoughts is primarily through reading the Word.

Hebrews 4:12 describes the Word as sharper than a two-edged sword that discerns the thoughts and intentions of our hearts. It doesn't deal with symptoms, it cuts right to the root of any issue we have. As we read His Word and submit to the leading of the Holy Spirit, it will cut away the things that are not like Him.

My hope for the next time you get confronted is that you will be able to clearly see your flawed perspective and then search the Word of God to find the solution. When we read the Word, we are encountering the presence of God, and when we are in His presence, we are changed. When we encounter Him, we step beyond pruning behaviors that might surface again later. In Him, we enter into truth and wholeness. John 8:32 says, "And you shall know the truth, and the truth shall make you free."

The ultimate truth we must all experience is seeing Jesus's sacrifice as payment for whatever might lay at the root of our bad mindsets and behaviors. When we are able to see them bound to the Cross with Him, we will know the truth and experience the freedom He died to bring us into. Regardless of what issues we deal with or what we get confronted over, our primary desire should always be to be free. No issue, regardless of how familiar or comfortable it might feel, is worth holding onto when Jesus offers freedom.

The greatest gift offered through confrontation is encountering the truth of the Gospel in a greater way and entering into more freedom than we've ever experienced. When we see this as the fruit of confrontation, we won't hesitate to give or receive it. We'll be excited about the opportunity of greater freedom on the other side.

Chapter 5

Creating Relational Depth

The nature of relationships is the deeper they go, the greater the potential for weakness to be exposed. When weakness comes to light, healing and transformation can begin. Many people today think that a deeper relationship means less conflict. This is simply not true. Some of the deepest relationships I have are the ones that have gone through the most confrontation.

The more you grow in connection with someone, the more you'll be around them. The more you're around someone, the more you begin to see little things they do that are either unpleasant, unbiblical, or harmful. When it comes from the heart of love, confronting these things has the potential to bring a great amount of healing and transformation.

Everywhere our Grace Place community goes, people comment on the love and care that we show each other. They see the intentional gifts, the selfless love, and the commitment that we carry. What they don't see is the amount of conflict and resolution that happens through living closely together.

They aren't there for the late-night conversations between roommates or the team meetings where bad mindsets and actions are being confronted. They often see the product, but they don't see the process. Everyone desires to have relationships free of friction and conflict. However, most don't understand that the only way to get there is by working through issues causing friction and conflict.

A few years ago, I was conducting an interview with a student interested in living in our discipleship house. On paper, everything seemed perfect. He had all the right answers and, apparently, hardly any struggles. However, as we talked, I had this nagging sense that something was off. So, I decided to call him on it and see how he responded.

I said, "I'm going to be honest. This all seems too good to be true."

As I asked more questions, the real story began to come out. It turned out he had lied on his application and had attempted to cover up his real struggles to paint himself in a positive light. The real story was much different and his life was a mess. I told him that the fact he lied was a very big deal. Our ministry was not going to be a good fit for him if this was how he handled the reality of his struggles.

After our call, the student was upset. No one had ever talked to him that way in his entire life. He was used to having things easy and being able to get almost anything he wanted. He thought, *This is ridiculous. He must have an impossible standard. If I'm not acceptable, how could anyone be?* The story could have ended there. The student could have walked away offended, found another place to live, and that would have been that.

However, as he spent time with the Lord, He began to show him how much he needed to hear what I had said. The fact no one had ever spoken to him like that began to intrigue him. He began

Creating Relational Depth

to see that he had settled for a low standard of transparency and accountability. With the Lord's help, he began to recognize that he needed more of this kind of direct communication in his life.

A few days later, the student reached out to me and asked if we could meet again. This time, he was humble, apologizing for lying on his application and trying to hide his sin issues. He said, "Daniel, you are right. I am in a mess and I need help. I don't deserve to be in your discipleship ministry, and I certainly don't walk in a standard of excellence, integrity, and purity right now in my life. It is true that I do try to hide my flaws and that is wrong. Will you please reconsider allowing me to join this program?"

Based on his humility and openness in the second interview, I agreed to pray about it. About a week later, I called and told him I would be happy to have him live in our discipleship house that year. This student lived in our housing program for several years and went on to serve on our leadership team. Being willing to directly confront him during the interview process opened the way for a deeper relationship built on trust and honesty.

I met one of my spiritual sons on a mission trip I led to South Africa. If you have ever been on a mission trip with me, then you know that we have a lot of fun, but we also work very hard. We often serve morning, afternoon, and night.

After fourteen days of non-stop ministry, we arrived at the final hotel of the trip. I had to make a decision of who was going to room with me. When I went to decide, I heard the Lord tell me to choose him rather than someone else I knew better. I had barely connected with this guy at all, but I followed the leading of the Lord.

The Lost Art of Confrontation

Before we went to sleep that night, I felt led to ask him about his testimony. At first, he didn't answer me. The way he tells the story is that he was faking as though he were asleep so he wouldn't have to talk about it. I knew the Lord had prompted me to talk to him, so I asked again. Through our conversation that night, I discovered he had a crazy past, and that God had saved him dramatically.

After hearing his testimony I knew I was supposed to mentor him. When we returned to California, I began to meet with him. After one of our meetings, I asked to see the apartment he was staying in. I came in to find that he had no furniture besides the futon he was sleeping on, surrounded by piles of dirty clothes. At the time, his diet was also very unhealthy. After learning all of this, I began to help him.

Slowly but surely our connection deepened. I would confront him about the clothes he was wearing and how he needed to change his wardrobe. He was called to be a mature man of excellence and what he was wearing did not match that call. He changed the way he ate because I would confront him on how he was taking care of his body. The longer we knew each other, the more I was able to speak into issues in his life that were causing him pain and difficulty.

That said, mentoring him was no Hallmark movie. Because of his past, confronting him was not easy. He had learned to take care of himself from a young age and did not trust my advice. We would end up in long heated conversations where I would have to be very direct about the decisions he was making and how they were hurting him.

He would sometimes do the exact opposite of what I advised him to do, and then have to learn the hard way he was wrong. Through all the difficulty, he would eventually choose to receive

Creating Relational Depth

the correction and change the way he lived. Because of that, the man he is today is unrecognizable from the boy he was.

If I had not listened to the Lord and continued to confront him, I'm convinced he and I would have never gotten close. We would have never had this trust and friendship because true friendship is built on connection. Connection comes through love and honesty. You can't be honest with a friend and not want to address the problems in their life.

The point of sharing these stories is that being confronted often does not feel good in the moment. In fact, it might even hurt sometimes. However, confrontation is never meant to be the end of the story. It's not meant to be the thing that breaks down relationships, but, rather, what establishes them. Søren Kierkegaard said, "Adversity not only draws people together, but brings forth that inner beautiful friendship."

Anyone can be a good friend or good mentor when things are going smoothly. It is when adversity comes and we need to speak up that deep, long-lasting relationships are built. When we begin to see that confrontation is not fighting against the other person, but fighting *for* them, things begin to change. We will experience less resistance from others because they will know and understand we have their best interests in mind.

Contrary to popular belief, speaking up creates a sense of safety in our relationships, because both parties develop trust that if anything needs to be addressed, there is freedom to do so. Nothing is hidden.

Chapter 6

Grace to Change

2 Corinthians 9:8 says, " And God is able to make all grace abound toward you, that you, always having all sufficiency in all things, may have an abundance for every good work." Confrontation, like every activity in a believer's life, is an act of grace. We are imparted grace to have the boldness to speak the truth in love, but we are also imparted grace to change.

Some people think that impartation only comes through the laying on of hands. However, the moment you are confronted, impartation to change is released. You may have never seen that you could live without the issue that was confronted. Yet, the moment someone points it out, your eyes are opened and the grace to make the change is available.

There is a principle in life I have recognized—if you see something, you can have it. For example, you may not know how to preach the Gospel, but when you watch someone else preach the Gospel you gain an understanding of how to do it. This truth is found in 1 John 3:2 which says, "Beloved, now we are children of God; and it has not yet been revealed what we shall be, but we know that when He is revealed, we shall be like

Him, for we shall see Him as He is."

When we see Him, we become like Him. When we are confronted, we can see a different way to live. When you see that perspective, you can access the ability of God or *grace* to transform into something different.

Grace is God's supernatural empowerment to live just like Jesus did. Hebrews 4:16 says, "Let us therefore come boldly to the throne of grace, that we may obtain mercy and find grace to help in time of need." Mercy alone will not get you or anyone you're confronting out of the negative cycle they are in. They need the empowerment of God's grace to change.

If I refuse to confront someone I am limiting the work of grace in their life. So if I decide I don't want to say something to my friend about a harmful habit they have, they won't have the opportunity to grow and change.

One of the leaders on my team used to be very uncomfortable being confronted. Generally, he has a laid-back personality, but whenever he would get confronted, he would tense up. He would put up walls and try to defend his actions. Growing up, confrontation wasn't normal in his family. When it did happen, it was intense. Early on, the Lord told me that whenever he tensed up and became defensive to remind him that I loved him and was for him.

Transformation didn't happen all at once, but gradually, the conversations got easier and easier. Not only did it get easier for me, but his whole attitude toward confrontation began to shift. I knew the Lord had done a lot of work on his heart when, in the middle of being confronted about something, he got excited instead of intense.

He got excited because he could see how what I was bringing up had held him back. Addressing an issue meant that God was going to give him the grace to believe better and do something different.

This is how confrontation can be for all of us. We do not need to have intense, in-your-face, shouting matches or battles. Just like what happened with the leader on my team, we can get to a place where we are *excited* about confrontation because of the potential transformation the Lord can unleash in our lives.

The reason I am so passionate about speaking up and challenging others to speak up is so that people can grow, change, and be transformed. Every oak tree starts as an acorn, but if it's not planted, it will never have the chance to grow to its full potential. Our words of confrontation are like seeds that the Lord uses to bring about transformation.

There is one guaranteed way to ensure nothing ever changes in the lives of those you care about—say nothing. It's tempting to take a hands-off approach with people, passively hoping that the Lord will do something about their struggle. He will, but rarely alone. He's looking for partnership. He's not just wanting to do something, He's wanting *you* to do something. When you do, you will be surprised by how much grace will be released for transformation.

Part III

Confronting

"Therefore, having put away falsehood, let each one of you speak the truth with his neighbor, for we are members one of another."
- Ephesians 4:25

Chapter 7

Bringing Awareness

The next few chapters will be answering the question, *how do I practically confront someone? What does confrontation actually look like?* In a very practical sense, the goal of any confrontation is to bring awareness. Everyone has blind spots in different areas of their lives. When we speak up, we hold up a mirror for someone else to be able to see the places they were blind.

As I said early on in the book, this does not mean yelling or intensity. More often than not, confrontation begins with simple questions, like, "Hey, is everything okay? You seem off. Hey, when you said that, what did you mean? Hey, I noticed you doing this behavior, is that normal for you?"

If you notice, none of these questions are intense. Through questions like these, you are bringing awareness that something might be off. It gives them an opportunity to check to make sure everything really is okay.

You might ask, what kinds of things should I be confronting? The best answer is anything that seems off. It's always better to lean on the side of saying something rather than staying quiet. Again, this doesn't mean we have to be a jerk or intense about it.

It's better to ask questions than make statements.

Often, out of discomfort or insecurity, we let things slide for a long time before speaking up. When we do this, we are bottling up our true feelings and creating unnecessary pressure in our relationships. When we finally do speak, words and emotions spew out of us like soda from a bottle that's been shaken. When we live this way, any confrontation—even small, miniscule things—feels like a massive deal when it's really not. As we learn to confront more often, our relationships will become pressure-free.

When confronting someone, always stick to the facts. Make observations without making judgments. Observation says, "I noticed you did this thing." Judgment says, "This is why you did it." Sticking to the facts frees us from making any judgments about what is going on beneath the surface. Notice the difference between these two questions.

"Hey Brian, have you noticed that you've been leaving dirty dishes in the sink?" "Hey Brian, could you stop waiting for other people to clean up after you and pull your own weight?" The first question doesn't assume to know why Brian is leaving his dishes out. It's simply asking a question based on a factual observation. The second question makes judgments about Brian's motives, that he likes other people cleaning up after him and that he doesn't pull his own weight.

Did you also notice how the second question has a harshness that the first question does not? It is an unsympathetic response that really has no place in any kind of friendship. When our attitude comes across as unnecessarily harsh, it's usually an indicator of an area where we are condemning ourselves. The measure of kindness or harshness with which we treat ourselves is often the same measure we will give to others. This is why it's important that we always deal with what's going on in our own hearts before trying to help someone else.

Relying on our own judgments and assumptions actually blinds us from seeing a different side of the story. Instead of helping someone else see the light, we darken our own vision of the situation. This is why Jesus told us in Matthew 7 to take the plank from our own eye before helping our brother get the speck of dust out of his. You must see clearly to be able to help someone else see. Otherwise, we're the blind leading the blind.

When I confront someone, I have made a discipline of not assuming I really know what's going on. Sometimes people can perceive this as patronizing, but I want to make sure that I'm not coming to the conversation with any bit of judgment or accusation.

Revelation 12:10 describes the Devil as "the accuser of our brethren." Any time we make an assumption as to why someone is doing something, we are accusing them. If we're accusing them, we're partnering with the accuser of the brethren. I don't know about you, but I don't want to give the devil any foothold in my life. Especially because partnering with accusation often causes defensiveness and separation rather than closeness and connection.

On top of accusation and judgment being a tool of the enemy, it is also not our right to say why someone is or is not doing something. Making assumptions makes people feel like you're talking down to them rather than helping them. If you find yourself making a lot of judgments, asking questions before you jump to a conclusion will help you tremendously. You'll also find that people are much more receptive to you. Oftentimes times the person will receive what you have to say, and though it may be difficult, they will be inspired to grow.

Sometimes when you confront someone, they might try to turn the conversation around on you. Let's take the confrontation I mentioned before as an example. What would happen if while addressing Brian's habit of leaving dirty dishes in the sink, he said to you, "You're talking about my dirty dishes, well how about you leaving your piles of laundry in the laundry room?" He may be right, but that isn't what's being addressed in the moment.

Healthy confrontations address one issue at a time. It's not the time to air out all your grievances with each other. The healthy response is to own what you did wrong, apologize, and clean up the mess you made.

When you address one issue at a time, people you're confronting will know they won't be blasted for everything they've ever done wrong. If you have multiple grievances with someone, it oftentimes means you haven't been addressing issues as they come up.

As you've been reading this, you may have had multiple issues come to mind that you need to address with someone. List them out and begin praying about what you should address first. As you address one issue, pray and ask the Lord for the next to bring up. The goal of our confrontation is not to overload someone with everything we see at one time. This isn't thinking of the other person. It's thinking of yourself.

Remember, confrontation is all about love. We bring things up to help others grow and to express concern for them. When you remove judgment and accusation, replace it with questions, and address the facts, you empower the love of God to flow through your relationships. This is how unity is formed. The sooner you confront a problem, the sooner you both have the opportunity to grow closer together.

Chapter 8

What to Do When Confronted

Proverbs 12:1 says, "Whoever loves discipline loves knowledge, but whoever hates correction is stupid." Nobody wants to be thought of as stupid or foolish, however, when we refuse to allow people to bring correction to our areas of weakness, we are inviting foolishness into our lives.

This is why maintaining a heart posture of humility is vital when being confronted. Humility comes from seeing that every good thing we have in life is a gift from the Lord. We owe Him everything and, therefore, claim no goodness in our own ability. When we walk in humility, it's easy to admit when we're wrong. Our identity, success, and significance are not tied up in being seen as "right."

For this reason, pride is the enemy of all growth and development. You cannot grow when you think you don't need anyone or have no areas to grow in. Pride says, *If anyone has a problem with my actions, that's their issue, not mine.* When we see ourselves as being superior or above the correction of others, we'll naturally try to defend ourselves and our actions.

Humility opens us to heart transformation, where, at best, pride will lead to behavior modification. A person who constantly makes mistakes, but owns up to them with humility, recognizes their need for the Lord. They will always end up further ahead in life than a person who pridefully goes his own way but outwardly performs much better.

You might ask, when someone confronts me, what does it look like to respond with humility? First, admit that you're wrong. This is not the moment to confront the confronter about some things that have been bothering you. As I said in Chapter Seven, ownership and respect look like listening and hearing them out without turning things around on the other person. Wait until the issue gets resolved and you've cleaned up your mess.

Always seek first to understand what the person confronting is saying. If we don't understand what we did wrong or how it affected other people, ask, "What about what I did do you think was off?" "How would you have handled this situation differently?" These kinds of questions create conversation and allow you to get understanding.

Secondly, apologize and ask forgiveness. I teach everyone I disciple not just to say "sorry" but to say "I am sorry." Simply saying "sorry" and moving on is like brushing aside what the person said. It is the least amount of ownership someone can take. Saying "I am sorry" feels like a small change, but it communicates that we are taking responsibility for our actions and also how they affected the other person.

When we say, "Will you please forgive me," we are recognizing that our actions affected our relationship with the other person. Seeking forgiveness is key because forgiveness releases you. When forgiveness is released, the standard is reset and the relationship is restored. A true apology contains

What to Do When Confronted

both these aspects, admitting we are sorry for what we did and seeking forgiveness.

Thirdly, explain how we're going to change. This is important because it helps us think through what we did and what we should do differently next time. This also communicates that we value the other person enough to let them know what to expect from us in the future. Then, they can help hold us accountable for what we say.

Finally, thank them for pointing out the issue. We could have continued to walk around blind, but thank the Lord that we have someone who cares enough about us to call us out! This also communicates that we appreciate the fact they spoke up. This is a key to establishing a culture of confrontation.

You might ask, what do I do if I don't agree with what the person is confronting me over? If you do not agree, humility asks, *Could I be the one wrong in this?* Proverbs says wisdom and victory are found in the multitude of godly counselors (see 11:14, 15:22, 24:6). It is wisdom to trust the perspectives of the godly men and women the Lord has surrounded us with.

Relationally speaking, trust is the ultimate goal of any confrontation. When someone corrects you and you grow from it, trust is developed. With each confrontation, deeper bonds form. The more we are confronted—and respond with humility and openness—the deeper and stronger our connections will be with those around us.

You might ask, what do I do if we just can't seem to agree? There are times when I have genuine disagreements with someone. We may have both been humble, seeking to understand, and wanting the best for one another. When we got to the root, we found that we simply didn't agree. This could be for a few reasons.

There might be times when you are confronted where you take it to the Lord, and you find that the other person was off in what they were saying. Let me be clear. It's not your responsibility to apologize for things that are not mistakes. Not everything you're confronted over will always be valid.

Imagine you are praying for someone to be healed and a friend from a conservative background who doesn't believe in healing tries to confront you. It's not your responsibility to apologize for following the Lord and obeying the Word. In these situations, the other person needs to adjust, not you. They may not be willing to change their belief system, but it's important not to water down what you believe for the sake of their comfort.

Disagreements can happen over anything, not just doctrinal arguments. We always want to respond in humility, seek to understand, and take what the person says to the Lord. However, our ultimate goal is to walk in truth and freedom. If what someone says does not align with the Word, it is our responsibility to stand firm. Confrontation is not about yielding to the preferences or comfort of another, but instead, working together to call each other to God's highest.

Another reason for disagreement might be because we have differing standards. To clarify, I'm not talking about whether Jesus is the only way to the Father or whether homosexuality is a sin. If someone is preaching heresy, we have a responsibility to speak against it. When talking about differing standards, I'm referring to how things should be done.

As you will notice in my books *The Lost Art of Excellence* and *It Is Finished*, most of my confrontations are correcting issues surrounding low standards, character, holiness, and purity. I don't find the need to split hairs on minor doctrinal differences such as whether you believe in portals or whether the forbidden fruit was an apple. I want to address the fear, pride, and condemnation that keep us from being all God called us to be.

For a long time, I ran housing for students who came from all over the world. There were many different family backgrounds and dynamics, and lots of opinions on what "cleanliness" meant. Some people came from families where having dishes in the sink was normal. Others came from a house where the countertops were spotless and there were rarely dishes in the sink.

In this case, the person who came from the house where everything was spotless would likely confront the others in the house not upholding the same standard. At the core, they may not agree on the standard of cleanliness. This is not the time to "agree to disagree." The person being confronted for leaving dirty dishes in the sink needs to raise their standard. Just because many conversations need to be had about the same issue doesn't mean the conversation isn't worth it. Some might perceive this as needlessly arguing. Yet, it's always worth the time it takes to come to a mutual understanding—regardless of how many confrontations it takes.

You might be tempted to think that because I have written a book on confrontation, I enjoy confronting people. In the past, I have had people ask me if I like having hard conversations. To many people's surprise, I actually don't enjoy conflict or confrontation. I have a massive value for fun and would much rather be laid back. However, I greatly value confrontation because it is the doorway to the growth of a relationship and holds up the standard of truth.

The Lost Art of Confrontation

The more we see conflict as a divider or disrupter of relationships, the less we will want to engage with it. When we begin to see adversity as a way for other people to grow, for friendships to deepen, for truth to be established, and for the Lord to do His work, the more we will desire to address conflict head-on.

We must ask ourselves, "How will they know to do any different if no one ever says anything?" and "If I see this is an issue, and I love them, why would I not say something?" When we begin to think this way, we won't allow ourselves to continue choosing the easier path. We will fight past comfort and inconvenience, and see the Lord use our words to bring lasting transformation.

Chapter 9

No One-Size-Fits-All

Confrontations come in all shapes and sizes. No two are the same because no two situations are exactly the same. We might have the same friend in common, but how I address things with them is different than how you would. What I hope this book has provided for you is the basic principles and guidelines that can help you no matter who you are talking with or what you need to address.

We get ourselves into trouble when we try to make formulas that apply to different types of people or situations. *I talk to this group of people this way and this group of people over here this way.* This is dangerous, unbiblical, and conceited.

We can't treat people differently based on their money or status. Nobody likes being treated like a celebrity. No one wants a "yes" man. You can never be a good friend to someone if you value them for what they *have* over who they *are*.

If I address things with one person based on a formula that worked for someone else, not only am I not following the Holy Spirit, but I am also not showing value for our relationship. We must be able to discern the difference between people and be able to ask the Lord "What does this person need?" Let me illustrate.

Let's say that you know three people who all committed the same sin and should be confronted. One flips burgers at McDonald's, one works for a local ministry, and one is a millionaire investor. Who would you feel the most comfortable confronting?

If you're like most people, the one that would feel the easiest would be the one who works at McDonald's. Why? He doesn't have much money. You'd probably find it more challenging to confront the person working for the local ministry, but most would feel very uncomfortable confronting the investor.

We can't make decisions on how to approach people based on outward appearances. Three people might have similar pasts, but different personalities. How we deal with each one depends on the state of their heart, and only the Lord can lead us in discerning what each person needs in the moment.

One of the most common questions I get whenever I teach on confrontation is, "How do I grow in discernment?" Discernment is such a valuable gift when addressing issues and helps get down to the root of things much quicker. You grow in it just like any spiritual gift—by using it! Most gifts start small and develop as we practice with them.

Starting out, you might only discern if a situation feels "weird." However, the more you call out when things feel weird or off, you'll learn when you're right and when you're wrong. You'll begin to recognize the Holy Spirit speaking more clearly and will be less reliant on outward appearances.

Many today have become hyper-critical of worldly people in the name of discernment. We must be cautious that we are not being more critical of sinners who do not know God than we are with believers. It is sadly common for well-intentioned church bodies to be harsher on the world for being lost in sin than they are on their own. This is the opposite of what Scripture teaches.

> *"It isn't my responsibility to judge outsiders, but it certainly is your responsibility to judge those inside the church who are sinning. God will judge those on the outside; but as the Scriptures say, 'You must remove the evil person from among you.'"*
> *- 1 Corinthians 5:12-13 NLT*

In this scripture, Paul is inviting us to deal with the issues in our own communities. He goes as far as to say that judgment for those outside of the Body of Christ is God's job altogether. If we treat an unbeliever the same as a believer, it's like trying to hammer a nail with a drill—it just doesn't work.

How do we confront a believer in sin? First of all, we can be hard on sin and simultaneously loving towards the person we're confronting. When we come gently to confront someone, we invite them into repentance and restoration.

Matthew 18:15-17 is an excellent example of how to confront a believer practically. If someone sins against you, let them know one-on-one what they've done wrong. If you confront them, but they still don't agree with you, don't stop there. It's best to bring another person or two into the conversation. If the person still doesn't agree with what you and the others are saying, take them to the whole church.

If they still refuse to listen, Jesus is clear on how we should handle this. Treat them like a Gentile or tax collector by removing them from the body. Even in this place of removing them from fellowship, the intention is still that they would one day come to a place of repentance. If someone comes back repentant and looking to change, I've never seen them rejected.

I have often noticed that we as believers are very sharp towards unbelievers and sinners. We get angry at the fact that they are sinning. However, we don't usually get mad at a dog for barking and wagging its tail, nor do we get frustrated that a leopard has spots. So why do we get angry and condemn a sinner when it's in their nature to sin?

Jesus was given plenty of opportunities to condemn sinners. Being the Son of God, he had every right to judge. However, time and time again, he chose mercy, forgiveness, and love. When the woman at the well was thrown before Him, having been caught in the very act of adultery, He declared, "Neither do I condemn you; go and sin no more" (John 8:11). Even when hanging on the Cross, He called out to the Father asking forgiveness for those who nailed him there.

This doesn't mean that we let things slide or let people walk over us. We confront unbelievers based on the laws of the land they are under. If you are harassed at work and don't confront it, you are saying this is acceptable behavior. If they do it to you, they will likely do it to someone else. By not confronting the harassment, you allow it to continue. The way to stop this cycle of sin is to speak out against it and bring it to the proper authority. If you were to immediately address the harassment at work, report it to your boss, and document it with human resources, the person would be fired and the harassment would stop.

No One-Size-Fits-All

Sin unconfronted becomes sin in you. If you don't challenge something wrong done to you, you submit yourself to sin. If you submit to sin rather than stopping it, it will often show up in your life as well.

The reality of the Gospel is that we as believers find ourselves in a battle and are called to stand up for righteousness and push back against the darkness. What you don't confront you condone. When you don't take a stand against the schemes of the enemy attempting to work their way into society, you silently condone his actions. This is why it's so important that we speak the truth and make our voices heard.

Our actions speak louder than words. One of the best and loudest ways to make yourself heard is through where you spend your money. The saying goes, "Money talks" and it's true! We don't have to wait for election day to cast a vote. We get to vote every day with the dollars we spend and where we choose to spend it.

It might feel inconvenient to not be able to shop where everyone else shops or eat where everyone else eats. We in America are especially used to the convenience of having everything we want right now. We're not called to order our lives around on what is most convenient. We're called to think about what is good, noble, pure, holy, and true, and then act according to those things (Phil. 4:8).

In the short term, no type of confrontation is ever convenient. It's not convenient to call something out, address a problem, or make a stand. It will always be more convenient to be quiet than to speak—until it's not. We never want to get to the place where our silence costs us the freedom to speak up altogether.

The Lost Art of Confrontation

Our lives are not measured by the conveniences we choose or how easily we have it. Our lives are always determined by what we choose to believe and how our beliefs shape and mold our actions. The Great Commission says to go into all the world and make disciples of all nations. Nations aren't discipled and people aren't reached by those who choose to stay quiet. They are transformed when people, who have the option to remain silent, choose the more inconvenient path and speak.

Conclusion

"The thief does not come except to steal, and to kill, and to destroy. I have come that they may have life, and that they may have it more abundantly."

- John 10:10

The Lord's desire for all of us is to experience abundant life. John 10:10 tells us this is why Jesus came in the first place. God wants us to be prosperous in every area of life, not just in finances or health. A significant, and often overlooked, aspect of abundant life is living free. My question is this, how can we be truly free if we constantly hold ourselves back out of fear of what others might think or say?

People have asked me how I am so comfortable confronting. Why is it that speaking up comes easier for me than others? The simple answer is that because I have done it often, the Lord has delivered me of a lot of fear of what people think. One of the most repeated commands in Scripture is "Do not be afraid," and yet, one of the most prominent issues in the lives of believers today is fear. Fear is one of the main reasons many stay quiet when they're called to speak.

Think about what your life would look like if you weren't afraid. What issues have you not addressed that you would speak up about? What problems in the world would you like to confront? What would your relationships look like? How close do you think you'd be with people? How would you look at yourself? If you answer those questions honestly, you get a glimpse of God's amazing plan for your life. The good news is, He didn't give you that spirit of fear, but He gave you a Spirit of power, love, and a sound mind (see 2 Tim. 1:7). The time to live in fear is over.

You can speak up today! When you kick that fear out of your life and say what needs to be said, you're going to experience the true freedom that God designed for you. It's time for confrontation to become normal in the body of Christ again.

Proverbs 28:1 says, "The wicked flee when no one pursues, but the righteous are bold as a lion." It's time for the people of God to stop fleeing when no one pursues, and end the days of being the silent majority. Jesus is as bold as a lion, and He calls us to embrace His righteous boldness.

When asked how to learn to pray, monk and theologian, Thomas Merton said, "You learn to pray by praying." In the same way, the way to learn to confront is through confronting. The only way to grow comfortable doing anything is through repetition and practice. At first, you probably won't do everything perfectly. You might feel a little awkward or nervous—not sure of exactly what to say—however, as you continue to speak, confidence will come. Any time you partner with the Lord to speak up for the truth, the Lord is faithful to give you the words to say.

Every believer is part of the family of God. In a healthy family, everyone has a part to play. When one person is low, the others are there to pick them up and encourage them. Families aren't perfect, but they are held together by a bond of love and commitment. We, as His family, need to develop into

Conclusion

a community where everyone is fighting for everyone. It's time we start fighting *for* one another rather than fighting *against* one another.

Confrontation is so vital because it is one of the primary methods we use to fight for each other and stand against darkness. It's only as we fight for the best of the people around us that the whole Body of Christ can be built up into what we are called to become. None of us are exempt from the process and every voice is necessary.

Each one of us needs to be heard, both within our churches and within our culture. It's time that speaking up becomes normal again. We need to accept the call to be bold witnesses for Christ. It's time for the Lost Art of Confrontation to be found.

About Grace Place

Grace Place Ministries is a discipleship community fueled by a passion to see God's people walk out their identity in Christ and establish His Kingdom upon the earth. We are committed to developing mature Christian leaders through one-on-one mentoring, building family through weekly gatherings, and providing leadership opportunities designed to facilitate connection and growth. We travel frequently to minister around the world and create resources to build up the Church in her righteous identity.

Vision

Mature sons and daughters
established in their identity in Christ,
spreading the Gospel of grace and truth.

Mission

Disciple young adults.
Minister around the world.
Resource the nations.

Discipleship is our Mission; Will you Join Us?

Now, more than ever, the body of Christ needs to arise and shine. The world is searching for answers and is in need of an encounter with God's love and truth. Who will raise up a generation to bring answers our world is desperately seeking?

"For the earnest expectation of the creation eagerly waits for the revealing of the sons of God."
— Romans 8:19

Whether it is a young man or woman needing a mentor or an entire church seeking the resources to disciple their community, you can make an impact!

Become a Partner with Grace Place Ministries:

Go to:
WWW.GRACEPLACEPARTNER.COM

Grace Place Ministries

Additional Resources

The Lost Art of Discipleship
God's Model for Transforming the World

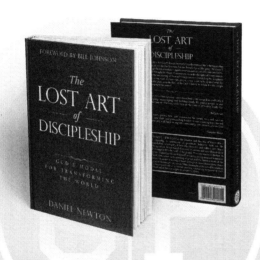

Discipleship is not a man-made idea. It is God's design for world transformation. *The Lost Art of Discipleship* is the uncovering of heaven's blueprints for remodeling the kingdoms of the earth into the Kingdom of our God. In his cornerstone book, Daniel Newton pulls from 20 years of experience in discipleship. As you read, prepare your heart to be ignited with the fires of revival that once swept the globe as in the days of the Early Church. It is time for the people of God to arise and shine for our light has come!

Available at www.GracePlaceMedia.com

@GracePlaceDiscipleship

Additional Resources

The Lost Art of Discipleship
Workbook

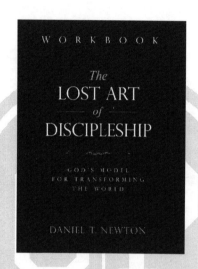

Enrich your understanding and increase your mastery of God's model for world transformation. This companion workbook to *The Lost Art of Discipleship* book is filled with exclusive content, in-depth exercises, and practical coaching to introduce a lifestyle of discipleship in your day-to-day walk. Whether you have been following the Lord for years or recently surrendered your life to Jesus, this manual breaks down the Great Commission and equips you for a life of fruitfulness!

Available at www.GracePlaceMedia.com

@GracePlaceDiscipleship

Additional Resources

The Lost Art of Discipleship
Online Course

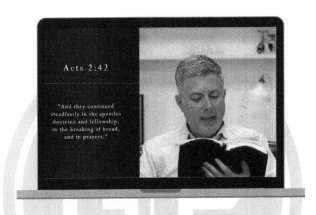

You can live the Great Commission. Every believer is called to embrace Jesus' final command: to make disciples... and this interactive online course is designed to take you even deeper into the rich content taught in *The Lost Art of Discipleship*.

Whether you are wanting to position yourself as a son or daughter, lead as a father or mother, or create a culture of discipleship, this course is for you! Rediscover the lost art with over five hours of video content, practical teaching, quizzes, and supernatural activations from Daniel Newton.

Available at www.GracePlaceMedia.com
@GracePlaceDiscipleship

Additional Resources

Immeasurable
Reviewing the Goodness of God

You are made in the image of the Miracle Worker, designed to manifest His glorious nature. *Immeasurable: Reviewing the Goodness of God* is a collection of 100 real-life stories of salvation, healing, deliverance, signs and wonders, reconciliation, and provision. Every miracle is a prophetic declaration of what God wants to do in, through, and for someone just like you.

Available at www.GracePlaceMedia.com
@GracePlaceDiscipleship

Additional Resources

Truth in Tension
55 Days to
Living in Balance

Never Give Up
The Supernatural Power of
Christ-like Endurance

Other Titles

The Lost Art of Perseverance
Rediscover God's Perspective on Your Trials

All Things
Have Become New, Work Together for Good, Are Possible

It Is Finished
Exposing the Conquered Giants of Fear, Pride, and Condemnation

The Lost Art of Faith Righteousness
Rediscover How Believing Leads to Receiving

The Lost Art of Fasting
Cultivating a Deeper Hunger for God

The Lost Art of Selfless Love
Freely Receive. Freely Give.

The Lost Art of Rest
The Only Thing Worth Striving For

The Lost Art of Excellence
The Supernatural Character of Christ

The Lost Art of Friendship
God's Design for Authentic Connection

Available at www.GracePlaceMedia.com

@GracePlaceDiscipleship

Additional Resources

GP Music: Beginnings

Everyone has a story. Most people don't realize that God doesn't just want to improve their story. He wants to rewrite it. Beginnings offers a fresh start, a new focus. This worship album invites you into the core anthems of grace and truth which have impacted us at Grace Place.

Our prayer is that this album helps you lay down your past mistakes, your present circumstances, and your future worries in order to lift both hands high in surrender to the One you were created to worship. We ask that you join us in a new beginning — an exciting start to a life filled with perseverance, focus, and surrender.

Available at www.GracePlaceMedia.com

@GracePlaceDiscipleship